THIS IS A CARLTON BOOK

New Woman trade mark © 2006 Emap Consumer Media Limited
Text copyright © 2006 Carlton Books Limited and Emap Consumer Media Limited
Design and artwork copyright © 2006 Carlton Books Limited

This edition published in 2006 by Carlton Books Ltd
A Division of the Carlton Publishing Group
20 Mortimer Street
London W1T 3JW

A CIP catalogue for this book is available from the British Library.

ISBN 13: 978-1-84442-290-6
ISBN 10: 1-84442-290-9

Editorial Manager: Roland Hall
Senior Art Editor: Zoe Dissell
Design: Sooki Choi
Production: Claire Hayward
Illustrations: Sarah Nayler

CARLTON
BOOKS

NEWWOMAN

Bloke Jokes

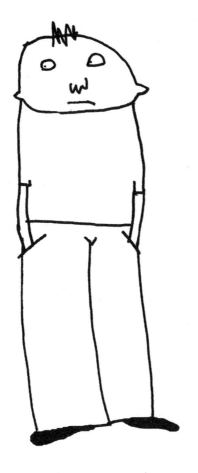

...Because Men Are
Funny Wherever You Are

for **Beaches**

CONTENTS

1

BEACH BODIES –
ARE THEY LIKE?

Harsh things to **say** to your holiday **fling**...

Wow…but your feet are **so big**!

•

But it still works – right?

•

Are you **cold**?

•

Perhaps if we water it, it'll grow.

•

How about a swim in the sea instead?

•

A lot of people **have surgery for that**.

So why is
God
punishing me?

I've never seen
one like that
before…

•

Maybe it
looks better
by daylight.

•

So I
guess I'm the
early bird!

Holiday
romance?

A couple are having a huge row on the beach when things get personal. 'I don't know why you wear a bikini,' says the bloke. 'You've got nothing to put in there!' The woman stares at him in amazement: **'Well, you're wearing trunks, aren't you?'**

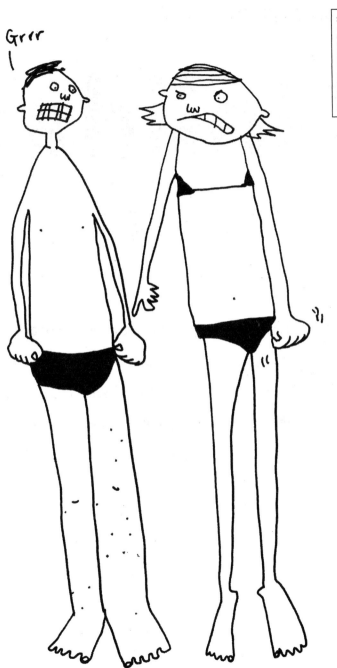

A bloke and a woman are taking a **romantic stroll** across **a moonlit beach**. Tenderly the bloke takes the woman's hand and asks her to **close her eyes**. He then places her hand **on his crotch**. To which she retorts: 'No thanks, I've **given up smoking**!'

'I wanted **sex**
with a **fitter**, more
attractive man so
I signed my husband
up for a week's
water-skiing lessons.'
'Is it working?'
'Oh yes – he water-skis
every day and
while he's there,
the **younger**, **fitter**,
more **attractive**
instructor
comes round to
my hotel.'

A
bloke
and a
woman
are on their
first holiday
but it's
slightly
tense...

Bloke: **'If your tits were a bit firmer, you wouldn't need that bikini top.'**

Woman: **'If your cock was slightly firmer, I wouldn't need your brother.'**

How do you spot a man with five willies?

His trunks fit like a glove!

How do blokes exercise on the beach?

Each time a bikini goes by, they suck in their stomachs!

What have you got if you have 100 blokes buried up to their necks in sand?

Not enough sand.

What happens when a bloke eats a mosquito?

He has more brain cells in his stomach than in his head.

How do you make seven pounds of fat very appealing to a bloke?

Put a nipple on it!

Why?

Why are all the **blokes** on this beach **sensitive**, **caring** and good-looking?

They all have boyfriends already.

Why are blokes like **bananas?** The older they get, the less firm they are.

●

Why are blokes like **cool bags?** Load them with beer and you can take them **anywhere.**

Why are **blokes** like ice creams?

**They're smooth, sweet
and usually head
right for your
hips.**

Why do blokes get married?

So they don't have to hold their stomachs in anymore.

●

Why are blokes like surf boards?

They're easy to ride once you get the hang of it.

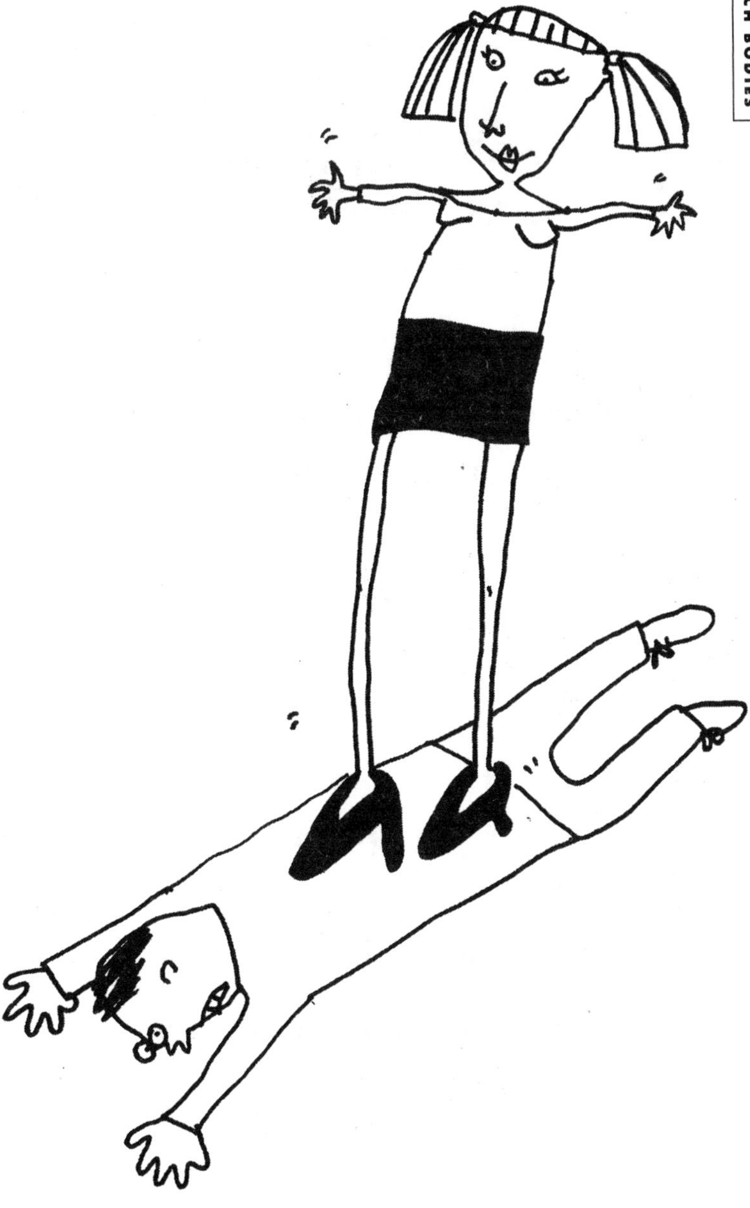

Beach
babes...

Two blondes walk
into a tourist office.
**You'd have thought
one of them would
have seen it!**

How do you tell the
difference between a
blonde
and a pair of sunglasses?
**The sunglasses sit
higher on your face.**

Why did the blonde have
sunglasses
inside her bikini knickers?
**The weather forecast
said sunny periods.**

Why are
blondes
like beer bottles?
**They've both got
nothing but air from
the neck up.**

What's the
difference between a
clever blonde
and a dumb blonde?
**Clever ones have
the dark roots
showing.**

A bloke is stranded on a beach with Pamela Anderson. Out of sheer loneliness the relationship becomes physical. For four months they have fabulous sex. One day, the bloke says to her, 'Can I borrow your eyebrow pencil to draw a moustache on you?' 'I guess so,' says Pamela. 'And would you wear some of my clothes and allow me to call you Ben?' he asks. Reluctantly she agrees. Then he grabs her by the arm and says,

'Hey, Ben, you won't believe who I've been sleeping with these last four months!'

How do you drown a muscle man?

Place a mirror in the hotel pool!

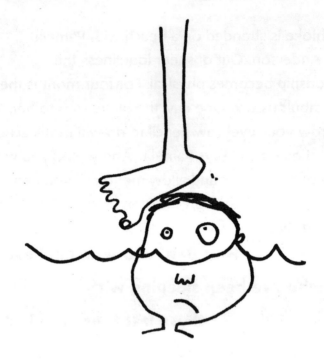

How
do you
stop a bloke
from drowning
in the sea?

**Take your
foot away
from his
head.**

How do you get a bloke in shape before you go on **holiday?** Keep putting the remote control between his **toes.**

Naked
lunch

How do you spot the most popular bloke on the nudist beach?

He's the one who can carry a cup of coffee in each hand... as well as a dozen doughnuts!

And who's the most popular girl on the nudist beach?

The one who can eat the sixth doughnut!

How do you spot a blind man on a nudist beach?

It's not so hard . . .

A bloke has been sunbathing too long and has got badly sunburnt, so he goes to the doctor's. After examining his whole body, the doctor says, 'Yes, it's definitely severe sunburn. I'll write you a prescription.' Checking to see what the doctor has prescribed, the bloke is surprised to see he's written down calamine lotion and Viagra. 'That's strange,' says the bloke. 'I can see the need for calamine, but why Viagra?' And the doctor replies, 'That's to keep the sheets off you at night!'

A bloke decides to go on a round-the-world cruise. At every port he sends his granny a beach photo of himself, but one of the destinations is a nudist beach. He decides to have the photo taken anyway and cuts it in two. But two days later he's horrified when he realizes he's sent his gran the wrong half of the photo, so he rings her to try and explain what's happened.

'Gran, did you get my last photo?' he asks.

'Yes, dear,' she replies. **'But you really should change your hairstyle –**

this one makes your nose look huge!'

Two **nuns** are **relaxing** on the beach when a **streaker** runs past. One has a **stroke**, but the other one **can't reach**.

What's the difference between an **ice cream** and a **masochist**?

An ice cream's often licked but never beaten...

2

NITE FEVER – HOT SPOT POT SHOTS

Hard things for blokes to say when they're drunk…

- **Innovative**

- **Preliminary**

- **Proliferation**

- **Cinnamon**

Very hard things for blokes to say when they're drunk…

- **Specificity**

- **British Constitution**

- **Passive-aggressive disorder**

- **Transubstantiate**

Downright impossible things for blokes to say when drunk...

- **Thanks, but I don't want to sleep with you.**
- **Nope, no more booze for me.**
- **No kebab for me – thank you.**
- **Oh, I just couldn't – no one wants to hear me sing.**
- **No, I won't make any attempt to dance, thanks. I have zero coordination.**

A couple are sitting in a bar when the bloke sees an advert for alcopops showing a bare-chested hunk complete with six-pack. 'Yeah, right,' says the bloke sarcastically. 'So if I drink ten bottles of that, I'll look like him, will I?' 'No,' replies his girlfriend. 'But when I drink ten bottles of that, you will!'

What's the best way to get a bloke to go clubbing?
Suggest he's too old for it!

What's the one thing all blokes in singles' bars have in common?
They're all married.

What do you call 200 blokes at the bottom of the ocean?
A great start!

How come
blokes
have such small balls?
So few of them can dance.

How do you
spot really

sexy

sandals?
**You can
get them
off with
one finger...**

What
do you
call 12
naked
blokes,
sitting on
each
others'
shoulders?
**A scrotum
pole.**

How
do you spot a
well-dressed bloke?
Easy...
His wife is good at
picking out
clothes.

What's the difference between a man and a holiday?

Nothing – because neither is ever long enough!

Size
matters…

Why do blokes
name their willies?
**Because it's always good
to be on first name terms
with the boss.**

Who's the
most popular guy
in the singles' bar?
The one in the corner,
licking his eyebrows.

What three words
do blokes most hate
to hear during sex?
Is it in?

What three words
do women most hate
to hear during sex?
Honey, I'm home!

A **bloke meets** a **girl** in a bar and they end up at her hotel. After a night of **torrid sex** the bloke wakes up and starts to get dressed. He notices a picture of a young and **fit bloke** beside the bed and he worries that this might be a **jealous boyfriend** or husband. As the girl wakes up, the bloke asks, 'Who's in the picture? It's **not your husband**, is it?' 'Oh no,' replies the girl. **'That's me before the operation!'**

Chat-up lines

'Hey, babe, what's your sign?'
'Do not enter!'

'So what do I need to say to seduce you?'
'Hi!'

What do I have to do to keep you interested in my company?
Own it!

You know, I like an intelligent woman.
Well, I've heard opposites attract.

Cutting put-downs for blokes who *really* deserve them:

I'll see you in my dreams…

if I eat too much cheese.

•

Darling, no one could

love you as much as you do.

•

There was something

I liked about you…

only you've spent it now.

**It's a shame
your parents didn't
practise safe sex.**

•

**Sleeping with you
has made me realize
how much I miss my ex.**

•

**You're proof enough
I can take a joke.**

Why?

Why are
blokes
like holidays?
**They never
seem to be long
enough.**

Why are
blokes
like lavatories?
**They're engaged,
vacant or
full of crap!**

Why are
blokes
like tapas?
**They satisfy you,
but only for
a little while.**

Why are
blokes
like cappuccino?
The best ones are rich, warm and can keep you up all night.

Why are
blokes
like bottles of ouzo?
Because they're both empty from the neck up!

Why
do women
need blokes?
Vibrators
can't buy the
next round.

Why did God invent alcohol?

So ugly blokes got a chance to have

sex!

Why did God create alcohol?

Because men fake foreplay.

Why do **black widow spiders** kill their males after mating?

To stop the snoring before it starts.

Why do men resemble cowpats?

The older they are, the easier they are to pick up!

Why's a hangover better than a man?

A hangover is usually gone by lunch time.

More put-downs for blokes who *really* deserve them:

You know you wanted
to make love
to me really badly?
Well, you've
succeeded!

•

You're depriving some
poor village
of its idiot.

I can't be your
type,
I'm not inflatable!

•

A
hard-on
doesn't count as
personal growth.

•

If I throw a stick,
**will you
leave?**

A club-owner has to
get rid of one of his staff.
He's narrowed it down to two:
Jack or Jill.
It's a hard decision as they're
both equally qualified and their
work is excellent. Eventually
he decides that next morning
whichever one drinks a glass
of water first will have to go.
Hung-over from all-night
partying, Jill arrives.
As she goes to the bar to get
some mineral water to take
with an aspirin, the club-owner
approaches her and says,
'Jill, I've never done
this before, but I have to
lay you or Jack off.'

Jill replies,

'**Could you jack off, I've got a terrible headache!'**

How do you know when you're using food as a substitute for sex?

You can't even get into your own pants.

The **medical-sounding**
notice that might just
stop your bloke
rolling in **drunk** at
3am **talking shite**:

WARNING:

Consumption of alcohol…

…**may** make you think you're whispering
when you're not.

…**may** cause you to thay shings like thish.

…**may** lead you to believe that ex-lovers are
dying for you to phone them at 4am.

…*may* leave

you wondering

what the hell

happened

to your trousers.

...*may* make you think you do indeed have mystical Kung Fu powers.

...*may* be the leading cause of inexplicable carpet burns on your forehead.

...*may* create the illusion that you're tougher, handsomer and smarter than some really, really big bloke called Baz.

...**may** cause a glitch in the space/time continuum, whereby small (and large) gaps of time disappear.

...**may** actually cause pregnancy.

...**may** make you think you can logically converse with members of the opposite sex without spitting.

…**may** cause you to roll over in the morning and see something really scary (whose species and/or name you can't remember).

…**may** lead you to think people are laughing *with* you, not at you.

3

CUNNING LINGUISTS – LANGUAGE LAUGHS

Two men wander into a café bar for lunch. One of them calls the waitress over and asks her for a 'quickie'. Not surprisingly, she slaps his face and storms off. His mate then says to him,

'It's pronounced "quiche".'

In a restaurant **a waitress** notices three Japanese blokes sitting at a table **masturbating**. 'What the hell are you guys doing?' she asks. '**I'm so sorry**,' says one of the blokes. 'But we're very, **very hungry** and we've been waiting here for an hour.' 'But what's that got to do with you three **jerking off**?' asks the waitress. The bloke replies, 'Menu say **"first come, first served!"**'

Heard about the blonde c h e f ?

She thought *coq au vin* was sex in the back of a transit!

A **bloke** walks into a bar and asks for a **double entendre**. So the landlady gives him one…

Money,
money, money…

Why did the Irish call their currency the 'punt'?
Because it rhymes with bank manager!

A bloke is drinking in a bar in Sweden.
A lovely woman sits down beside him.
'Hello,' he says. 'Do you speak English?'
'Oh, I speaking not much English,'
replies the woman.
'How much?' asks the bloke.
The woman replies, **'200 kronor!'**

A bloke visits a Parisian brothel one Monday evening. He has a great time and is surprised when he's handed 5,000 Euro as he leaves. Next evening he returns and the same thing happens again. He goes back the following night, but this time he doesn't receive a single cent and so he complains to the concierge. 'Why should we pay you?' asks the concierge. 'We don't film on Wednesdays!'

Travellers' tales

A bloke visits a Native American reservation. He notices a Chief wearing an unusual bracelet decorated with animal bones. Curious, he asks what this symbolizes. 'This humpaa bracelet,' replies the Chief. 'For every humpaa I screw, I get to add bone to bracelet.' 'I see,' says the puzzled anthropologist. 'But what exactly is a "humpaa"?' 'Humpaa is everywhere,' replies the Chief. 'Beaver is "humpaa". I screw beaver, I add to bracelet. Bear is "humpaa". I screw bear, I add to bracelet. Skunk is "humpaa". I screw skunk, I add to bracelet...' 'Oh dear,' says the bloke, embarrassed. 'No,' replies the Chief. 'Not "humpaa"! Never screw deer – their ass-holes too high and they run too fast!'

A man goes to Japan on holiday. On his first evening he meets a beautiful Japanese girl. Despite the language barrier, they end up in his hotel room. All night long they have the most amazing sex and every time he feels he can't go on any more, she shouts, 'Hitakushi! Hitakushi!' He's not sure what it means, but it sounds as though she's having a good time, so he feels a bit of a stud. Next day, tired but happy, he meets his mate (who happens to be Japanese) on a golf course. At the 18th hole his mate hits a hole in one. 'Hitakushi!' says the man. His mate looks very cross and shouts back, 'What do you mean, *wrong hole*?'

A woman meets a German in a club and goes back to his hotel room. He mentions he's a bit kinky and would she mind dressing up? She says no, so he gets out a big costume, covered in feathers, with a duck's bill and enormous webbed feet. She thinks this is OK, so she puts it on and they start shagging. He then asks if she would mind putting something else on, too, and gets out four huge bedsprings. She says OK, so he straps them onto her knees and elbows. She gets on all fours and soon they're at it, bouncing away, getting more and more excited. Finally, he asks her to shout 'Quack! Quack!' When she does this, they both have the most amazing orgasm. Still gasping, she asks, 'So how did you manage that?' 'Four-sprung duck technique!' he replies.

On holiday in France
a **woman** passes a
pet store and sees a sign:
'**Clitoris-licking** Frog'.
She goes in and says,
'I've come about the
clitoris-licking **frog**.'
The assistant answers,
'Oui, Madame?'

A man goes in to a Far East brothel and asks for their kinkiest girl. 'Sorry, sir, all our girls are busy, but if you like, you can have the pig.' He thinks this is pretty kinky, so he has sex with the pig. Next week, he returns, asking for their kinkiest girl. 'Sorry, sir, all our girls are busy.' 'Well, can I have the pig again?' 'No, sorry sir, no pig, but if you like you can go into the end room and watch.' He goes into the end room and there are a dozen guys, all masturbating, watching through a pane of glass as a woman licks melted chocolate off a man tied to the bed. 'Wow!' he says. 'That's pretty hot!' 'You think this is good,' says one of the guys. 'Last week some pervert was in there having sex with a pig!'

A young bloke is travelling across China when he comes to a house in the mountains. He knocks on the door and is greeted by an old man. 'I'm lost,' says the bloke. 'Can I stay for the night?' 'Certainly,' replies the old man. 'But on one condition... If you lay a hand on my beautiful daughter, I will inflict on you the worst Chinese tortures known to man.' The bloke agrees and he's invited to dinner. But the old man's daughter is incredibly beautiful and later on the bloke creeps into her room for a night of passion. At dawn, he goes back to his room to sleep. A little later he wakes and feels something pressing on him. He opens his eyes and sees a large rock on his chest with a note saying, 'Chinese Torture 1: Large rock on chest.' 'Well, if that's the best he can do,' thinks the bloke, 'I don't have much to worry about.' He gets up and throws the rock out of the window into a deep ravine. As he does so, he notices another note on the window frame. It reads, 'Chinese Torture 2: Rock tied to left testicle.' He looks down and sees his testicle is indeed tied to the falling rock. The bloke jumps out of the window in the hope of a soft landing to save his testicle. Suddenly he sees a third note pinned to the rope. As he falls, he reads, 'Chinese Torture 3: Right testicle tied to bedpost.'

On holiday in
Afghanistan a bloke
is surprised to see
the local men allow their
wives to **walk in front** of them.
He approaches a local and
remarks, 'I thought it was the
custom in Islamic countries
for wives to walk ten paces
behind their **husbands**?'
'It was,' replies the local,
'but the war changed things.'
'What difference did the
war make?' asks the bloke.

'Landmines!'

the local replies.

In the duty free lounge a blonde walks up to the perfume counter and picks up a sample bottle. She sprays scent on her wrist and smells it. 'That's lovely,' she says to the sales assistant, 'What's it called?' The assistant replies, 'It's "Viens à Moi", French for "Come to Me".' The blonde takes another sniff and says, 'That's strange – it doesn't smell like come to me!'

A bloke grabs a seat next to a gorgeous woman on a plane. He strikes up a conversation, but then she asks if he minds her reading her book.

Bloke: 'Not at all. What are you reading?'

Woman: '*The Joy of Sex.*'

Bloke: 'Anything interesting?'

Woman: 'Yes, apparently a man's nationality can indicate things about his penis size.'

Bloke: 'Like what?'

Woman: 'Well, Polish men have the longest ones and American Indians the thickest. Oh, by the way, my name is Laura Smith…'

Bloke: 'Good to meet you, Laura. Mine's Tonto Kawalski.'

In heaven, the **lovers** are **French**, the **comedians English** and the **engineers** are **German**. In hell, the **comedians** are **German**, the **engineers French** and the **lovers** are **English**!

What's the difference between men and fine French wine?

You don't have to roll a man around in your mouth to get the most enjoyment out of him!

The language of love. . .

- Wet dream – snoregasm
- Group sex – fourgasm
- Sex that goes on for hours and hours – soregasm
- Cheap sex – poorgasm
- Noisy sex – roargasm
- Sex on the beach – shoregasm
- Swedish sex – smorgasborgasm
- Sex on holiday – tourgasm

The night before her wedding an Italian bride-to-be asks her mother how she can make her husband happy. 'Well, there's all sorts of things a wife can do with her husband in bed,' replies her mother. 'Mama,' says the daughter. 'I know how to fuck! What I need is your lasagne recipe!'

An American, an Australian and a German bloke are on holiday and bragging about the length of their penises. They go to the top of a ten-storey block and take it in turns to flop their tackle over the side. The German goes first and dangles his penis down five storeys. It's the Australian bloke next and he manages eight storeys. Last, the American flops his penis over the side and starts frantically twitching his hips about. 'What are you doing, mate?' asks the Aussie.

'Dodging traffic!' replies the American.

4

HOTELS – CHECKOUT TIME?

A **blonde**, a **brunette** and a **redhead** walk into the lift in their hotel and notice a **white sticky patch** on the wall. 'Funny,' says the brunette, 'that looks like **spunk**.' The redhead sniffs the air and says, 'Yep, and it smells like spunk, too.' The blonde puts her **finger in** the sticky patch, **licks** it and says, 'Well, it's none of our **boyfriends**'!'

A **bloke** walks through a hotel lobby. He accidentally **bumps** into a woman and his elbow **digs** into her breast. 'Oh, sorry,' he says, 'but if your **heart** is as **soft** as your **breast**, I know you'll forgive me.'

The woman replies: 'And if your **penis** is as **hard** as your **elbow**, I'm in Room 12!'

A **bloke** books himself into a country **guesthouse** for the night. Next day he's getting packed when he finds he's desperate for a **crap**. Unfortunately the bathrooms in the corridor are all occupied. He can't wait so he's forced to crouch on the floor over a sheet of **newspaper**. But now he has the problem of hiding the **smelly turd**. He looks around and notices a **large pot** plant in the corner of his room.

He lifts the **plant** out of the pot, drops in the **turd** and pushes the plant down on top to disguise it. **Phew!** A week later he's back home when he receives a letter from the guesthouse. The letter reads: 'We know what you did. All is forgiven, but **PLEASE tell us where you hid it**!'

A bloke walks
into a bar...

A bloke walks into a hotel bar and asks for six double whiskies. The guy behind the bar looks shocked: 'That's an awful lot of whisky for someone who's come on his own.' 'But I've just had my first blow job,' replies the man. 'In that case have another one on the house,' offers the barman. 'Well,' says the bloke, 'if six doesn't take the taste away, I don't think the seventh one will work either!'

A bloke walks into a hotel bar with a giant cork shoved up his backside. The barman asks him what happened. 'Well, I was walking along the beach,' says the bloke, 'when I found a lamp, so I picked it up to brush off the sand and a genie popped out. The genie said I had three wishes, so I said, "Wow! No shit!"'

The local **stud** walks into a hotel bar and orders a **drink**. He looks worried and the barman asks what's wrong. 'An **unhappy husband** wrote to me and said he'd kill me if I didn't stop **screwing** his **wife**.' 'So why don't you just stop?' asks the bartender. 'I can't,' replies the stud. 'He **didn't sign his name**!'

A bloke walks into a hotel bar and sees a beautiful woman sitting alone. He goes over to talk to her. After a while he invites her back to his room. 'I can't,' says the woman. 'I'm saving my virginity until I meet a man I can truly love.' 'That must be hard,' says the bloke. 'Oh, it doesn't bother me too much,' says the woman. 'It's my husband who's really unhappy!'

A bloke walks into
a hotel bar and says
to the barman:
'An orange juice, please.'
'Still?' replies the barman.
'Well, I haven't changed
my fucking mind!'
replies the man.

A **man** walks into a hotel **bar**, meets a **woman** and they end up back at his room. 'You don't talk much,' she says as he's **undressing**. 'No,' he says, 'I do my talking with this.' '**Sorry**,' she says, 'I don't do small talk!'

Two blokes are **sitting** in a **hotel bar**. One says, 'I remember the first time I used alcohol as a **substitute for women**.' 'So what happened?' the other bloke asks. The first one says, 'I got my **knob stuck** in the neck of the bottle!'

A bloke is staying in a hotel. 'Will there be anything else, sir?' asks the bellboy, after setting out an elaborate dinner for two. 'No, thank you,' replies the bloke. As the bellboy turns to leave he notices a glamorous satin negligee on the bed. 'Anything for your wife?' he asks. 'That's a good idea,' says the bloke. 'Bring me a postcard!'

Chat-up lines?

Your room or mine?
Both, you go to yours and I'll go to mine.

•

I wish you were a hotel door –
I'd bang you all night.
**I doubt it; you haven't got a key
that would fit my lock.**

•

A glamorous blonde is staying at
an expensive hotel and decides to try a
milk bath. She calls down to reception and
asks them to send up 30 pints of milk to fill
the bath. 'Pasteurised?' asks the receptionist.
'Nah, just up to my tits!' she replies.

•

What do you call a woman who does
the same amount of packing as a bloke?
A lazy cow!

•

Dave walks into the hotel lounge and sees his mate Jeff huddled over a table, looking really sad. He asks what's wrong. 'Well,' replies Jeff, 'you know that lovely girl I wanted to ask out, but couldn't because I got an erection every time I saw her?'

'Yes,' replies Dave, smiling.

'Well, I finally plucked up the courage to invite her out and she agreed.'

'That's great,' says Dave. 'So when are you meeting her?'

'I went to her hotel room this evening,' says Jeff. 'But because I was worried I'd get an erection again, I got some sticky tape and taped my todger to my leg, so if I did, it wouldn't show.'

'Sensible,' says Dave.

'So I got there and rang the bell, but she answered it in the sheerest, tiniest dress you ever saw.'

'Fantastic! So what happened then?'

'I kicked her in the face!'

Couples

A **couple** are staying in a hotel with very thin walls and they're worried the neighbours will hear them **talking** in bed. 'I know,' says the woman, 'when you **fancy** sex, put your hand on my breast and **squeeze** once. If you don't want sex, squeeze twice.' 'OK,' says the man. 'If you want **sex**, put your **hand** on my penis and pull once. If you don't want sex, pull it 50 times!'

Some newly weds arrive at their honeymoon hotel and ask for a double room. 'As it's your honeymoon,' says the receptionist, 'wouldn't you like the bridal suite?' 'No, it's all right,' says the bridegroom. 'I'll just hold onto her ears until she gets the hang of it!'

A pair of newly weds are in their hotel honeymoon suite. The bloke removes his trousers, gives them to the girl and tells her to put them on. As they're four sizes too big, she says, 'There's no way I can wear these.' 'Good!' he says. 'Now you know who wears the trousers in this relationship.' Quietly, she removes her tiny knickers and says, 'OK, put these on.' 'I can't get into them,' says the bloke. She replies, 'Correct, unless you change your attitude!'

A couple have separate hotel rooms because of his loud snoring. One night, feeling amorous, the bloke calls out to his girlfriend: 'Oh, my little boopey-boo, I miss you.'

So his girlfriend gets up and goes to his room, but as she's walking in, she trips on the carpet and falls flat on her face.

'Oh,' he says sweetly. 'Did my little honey-woney hurt her ickle nosey-wosey?'

The woman picks herself up, gets into her boyfriend's bed and they make passionate love. Going back to her room afterwards she trips once again on the carpet and falls flat on her face. This time the bloke raises his head from the pillow, looks at his girlfriend lying there and says, 'Clumsy bitch!'

A bloke walks into his **hotel** room and discovers another **bloke** having **sex** with his girlfriend. 'What the hell are you doing?' he asks. His **girlfriend** turns to the other bloke and says, **'See, I told you he was stupid!'**

What should you say if a bloke
asks you: 'Am I your first?'
'You could be, you look familiar.'

A woman falls from the 23rd floor of a hotel. As she falls, she prays, 'God, please give me a chance to live!' Suddenly a bloke leans out of his balcony and catches her in his arms. Before she has a chance to thank him, he asks, 'Do you suck?' 'Of course not!' she shouts, thinking this can't be what God intended. So the bloke lets go and she hurtles toward the ground again. Suddenly a second bloke puts out his arms and catches her. 'Do you screw?' he asks. 'No!' she yells, wondering what on earth God is playing at, sending all these perverts to catch her. So the bloke drops her and she continues to fall. Just as death seems certain, a third bloke puts out his arms and catches her. Before he can say a word, the woman shouts, 'I suck, I screw!' 'Slut!' cries the man and drops her.

5

PLANES AND TRAINS – FLY HIM TO THE MOON, WHY DON'T YOU?

A number of planes are delayed at the airport because of bad weather and the airport hotel starts to get packed. It's so overcrowded that three blokes have to sleep together in the same bed. When they wake up the next day, the man on the right side of the bed says, 'I had a fantastic dream last night – I dreamt a lovely woman was jacking me off all night long.' 'That's strange,' says the man on the left. 'My dream was exactly the same.' 'You're disgusting,' says the middle bloke. 'I had a lovely dream – all about skiing!'

What's the difference between a cockpit and a box office?

A box office is a place that tries to ensure everyone has a satisfactory evening's entertainment, but a cockpit is only really concerned with getting up and down.

A bloke sits next to an attractive woman on the plane. To get her talking he asks if she'll play a game with him. She refuses so he tries again. 'What if I ask you a question and if you get it wrong you pay me a fiver. Then you ask me a question and if I get it wrong, I pay you £50?' She agrees so long as she can go first, then says, 'What goes up a hill red and comes down it blue?' With that she turns over to sleep. The bloke looks puzzled and spends three hours searching the Web on his laptop for the answer. Eventually he wakes her with the £50 and admits defeat: 'Well, what is it?' She takes a fiver from her purse, gives it to the bloke and goes back to sleep!

A bloke sits in the first class section on a plane to America, but his ticket is only economy class so the air hostess asks him to move. He refuses, saying: 'I have a good job and pay my taxes – I deserve to sit in first class.' After ten minutes of arguing, the chief air hostess comes over and asks him to move. He refuses, again saying, 'I've a good job and I pay my taxes so I deserve to sit in first class.' Ten minutes later, the pilot comes over, whispers in the bloke's ear and he moves and sits at the rear of the plane. When the hostesses ask the pilot what he said, he replies, 'I told him the front half of the plane doesn't go to America!'

A young **bloke** finds himself sitting next to an **old priest** on a plane, waiting for take-off. There's a minor technical hitch so the captain announces that the airline will serve a round of **free drinks** to make up for the delay. An attractive **air hostess** comes by to find out their order and the bloke asks for a **double Scotch**.

She then asks the priest what he'd like. 'Oh no,' he replies. 'I'd rather **commit adultery** than drink alcohol.' **Mid-swallow** and **dribbling** Scotch down his front, the bloke replaces his drink on the cart. 'Excuse me, miss,' he says. **'I didn't know I had a choice!'**

On a transatlantic flight the plane passes through a powerful storm. The turbulence is terrific and one wing of the plane is struck by lightning. One woman in particular loses it. Screaming, she stands up at the front of the plane. 'I'm too young to die!' she says, 'but if I have to die, I want my last minutes to be memorable! Although I've had plenty of lovers, no one's made me really feel like a woman. Is there anyone on this plane who can do this?'

Silence... everyone's forgotten their own peril. They all stare at the desperate woman. At the rear of the plane a man stands up. 'I can make you feel like a woman,' he drawls. He's gorgeous! Tall, muscular, with long, flowing blond hair and deep blue eyes. Slowly he walks down the aisle unbuttoning his shirt as he goes. No one moves. The woman breathes heavily in anticipation. He removes the shirt and his muscles ripple across his chest as he reaches her. He extends the arm holding the shirt to the trembling woman. Gently, he whispers,

'Iron this!'

Blokes are like trains –
**they always stop
before you get off!**

•

Most popular female fantasy?
**Sex with your boyfriend's
best friend, a film star
or a stranger on a train.**

•

Most popular male fantasy?
**Sex with a woman
who isn't fantasizing
about someone else!**

A
bloke gets
talking to a girl
on a train and asks
her name. 'I call myself
"Carmen",' she replies.
'It's not my real name, but it
reflects my two main interests
in life: fast cars and sexy men.
So what's your name,
handsome?' The bloke
reflects for a moment,
then says,
'Beerfuck!'

A man and woman are travelling together on a train. Suddenly the woman sneezes, starts to writhe around and moan, quivers all over, then goes back to her book. A few minutes pass and the same thing happens again: the sneeze, the writhing and moaning, then the quivering. 'Are you OK?' asks the man. 'Yes,' replies the woman. 'I must warn you, though, I have an unusual medical condition. Every time I sneeze, I have an automatic orgasm.' 'And are you taking anything for it?' 'Yes – pepper!'

A bloke staggers drunkenly into the back of a cab. He leans towards the driver and asks, 'Any room for a lobster and a bottle of wine on your front seat?' 'I think so,' says the driver. 'Good!' the bloke replies and promptly throws up.

On the beach three women are having a laugh comparing their boyfriends' lovemaking techniques to cars. The first says: 'My boyfriend's like a Rolls-Royce... sophisticated and comfortable.' The second says, 'Mine's like a Ferrari... fast and powerful.' The third says, 'Well, my boyfriend's like an old Morris Minor... you have to start him by hand and jump on when he finally gets going!'

What do fat blokes and mopeds have in common?
They're both a good ride but you'd die if your mates saw you on one!

•

What's the difference between a bloke and a motorbike?

1 You can tell how big the exhaust is before you start riding a bike.
2 You can swap bikes with your friend to see which is the better ride.
3 It's the motorbike that suffers if you don't use enough lubrication.
4 A motorbike stays between your legs till *you've* had enough fun.
5 You only chain a motorbike up when you've *finished* riding it.

And the difference is...

What's the difference between
a blonde and a 747?
Not everyone's been in a 747.

•

What's the difference between
a bloke and a luggage trolley?
**Sometimes a luggage trolley
has a mind of its own.**

•

What do bleached blondes and
jumbo jets have in common?
They both have a black box!

Chat-up
lines

We could be joining the Mile High Club
by midnight tonight.
We probably will be – but not with each other.

A bloke is driving up a steep, narrow mountain road in Spain. A woman is driving down the same road. As they pass each other, the woman leans out of the window and yells, 'Pig!'

The bloke automatically leans out of his window and replies, 'Bitch!'

They each continue on their way and as the bloke rounds the next corner, he crashes into a pig in the middle of the road.

If only blokes would listen…

A bloke visits Las Vegas on a gambling holiday, but it goes really badly for him. He loses all his money except one dollar and the return air ticket, but he knows if he can just get to the airport, he can make it home. Outside the casino is a cab, so the bloke explains his plight to the driver. He promises to send the money from home, gives him his address, his passport number, everything, but the driver just says: 'If you don't have the $15 fare, get out of my cab!' So the poor bloke hitchhikes to the airport and just catches his flight on time.

A year later, having worked really hard to rebuild his finances, the bloke returns to Las Vegas, figuring that this time he has to win. And he does – big time! When he leaves the casino for the airport, he sees the miserable cab driver at the end of a long line of taxis and plans his revenge. He gets into the first cab in the queue and asks how much to go to the airport. '$15,' is the reply. 'And how much for you to give me a blow job on the way?' he asks. 'Out of my cab!' screams the driver...

... The bloke gets into the back of every taxi in the long queue and asks the same question, getting exactly the same reply each time. But when he gets into the cab of his old enemy, he just asks, 'How much to the airport?' When the cab driver says, '$15,' he says 'OK.' As they drive past the long line of cabs, the bloke smiles broadly and gives a thumbs-up to the remaining cab drivers...

A bloke and a woman have a terrible car accident while on holiday. Both cars are demolished, but amazingly neither is hurt. The woman says, 'So you're a bloke? Interesting... I'm a woman. Wow, just look at our cars! There's nothing left, but we're OK. This must be a sign from God that we should meet, be friends and live together in peace.' Flattered, the bloke replies, 'Yes, I agree with you completely. It must be a sign from God.'

The woman continues, 'Here's another miracle. My car's completely demolished, but this bottle of wine didn't break. Surely God wants us to drink it and celebrate our good fortune.' She hands the bottle to the bloke. He nods in agreement, opens the bottle and drinks half, then hands it back. The woman takes the bottle, immediately puts the cap back on and hands it to the bloke. The bloke asks, 'Aren't you having any?' The woman replies: 'No, I think I'll wait for the police!'

6

SURF AND TURF – GIVE HIM A SPORTING CHANCE, NOT!

Chat-up lines...

Do you have any Irish in you?
Why, would you like some?

•

You. Me. Whipped cream. Handcuffs.
Any questions?

•

If it's true that we are what we eat,
then I could be you by morning.

•

Let's go back to my hotel and do
the things I'm going to tell people
we did anyway.

• One swallow doesn't make a summer,
but it can make a bloke's day!

• What's the worst part of a bloke's body?
**His penis – it has a head with no
brains, hangs out with two nuts and
lives round the corner from an asshole!**

• What's the thinnest book in the world?
What Blokes Know About Women.

How
do blokes'
brain cells
die?
Alone!

How is
a bloke
like the
weather?
**Nothing
can be
done to
change
either
one of
them.**

• Why are blokes like dolphins?
**Both are said to be intelligent,
but no one can prove it.**

• What should you do if your bloke walks
out? **Shut the door after him.**

A bloke visits Cuba for a week. The day before he leaves he still hasn't tried the local food so he goes to a restaurant, orders and then sees the bloke opposite him eating a delicious meal. He calls the waiter over and asks for the same meal, but there's none left. The bloke asks what it is and the waiter replies, 'That's the testicles from the bull that lost the fight earlier this morning. If you come back tomorrow, we'll make the same dish for you.' So the bloke goes back the next day and the waiter has his food prepared for him. He eats the meal and calls the waiter over: 'This meal was delicious, but it seemed a lot smaller than the one the bloke yesterday was eating.' And the waiter replies, 'Ah, sorry sir, sometimes the bull wins!'

A bloke is stranded on a desert beach for a whole year. One day an amazing brunette walks out of the sea dressed in scuba gear and lays down on the sand beside him. 'Cigarette?' she asks. 'Great,' says the bloke, amazed as she unzips her wetsuit pocket, produces a pack of Marlboro, lights it seductively and hands it to him. 'Incredible,' says the bloke as she unzips another pocket and produces a chilled can of Stella and two glasses, pouring them both a drink...

... The brunette
edges closer to the bloke,
presses herself up
against him, saying,
'Fancy fooling around?'
'Oh my God!'
cries the bloke, thinking
he's gone to heaven.
'Don't say you've got
a set of golf clubs
in there, too!'

A bloke goes into a supermarket and buys a tube of toothpaste, a bottle of Pepsi, a bag of tortilla chips and a frozen pizza. The cute girl at the register looks at him and says: 'Single, huh?' Sarcastically the bloke sneers: 'How'd you guess?' She replies: 'Because you're ugly.'

Still more
chat-up lines...

Fancy a quickie?
Can you *do* any other kind?

•

What's your sign?
Private property!

•

Is that a ladder in your stocking,
or a stairway to heaven?
**You have to be good
to get to heaven.
Really good!**

What's a nice girl like you
doing in a place like this?
**If I *were* a nice girl, do you
think I'd be in a place like this?**

So where have you been all my life? **Where I'll be for the rest of your life: in your wildest dreams!**

•

I can give you **supersex.** **I'll take the soup, thanks.**

•

I'm a magician – fancy seeing my wand? **Will it make you disappear?**

What's the
difference...

What's the difference
between a beach bar
and a clitoris?
**Most blokes have no
trouble finding the bar.**

•

What's the difference
between an attractive man
and an ugly one?
Ten shots of tequilla.

What's the difference
between a sea urchin
and a Porsche?

**A sea urchin
has pricks
on the
out-
side.**

•

What's
the difference
between a bloke
and a pig?

**A pig doesn't turn into a
bloke after two pints of lager.**

What's the difference between a bloke and a condom?
Condoms these days aren't thick and insensitive.

What's the difference between a golf ball and a G-spot?

Men will always look for a golf ball.

Perfect put-downs

• Save your breath –
you'll need it to blow up your girlfriend.

• If my dog looked like you, I'd shave its bum and
train it to walk backwards.

• I heard you're nobody's fool. Never mind,
perhaps someone will adopt you.

• Go out? Yes, we could visit the zoo.
They must be wondering where you've been.

Recipe for perfect happiness:

1 A man with a 12-inch cock who can satisfy you all night.

2 A caring man, who does all the housework and
waits on you hand and foot.

3 A rich man who showers you with presents.

4 Making sure 1, 2 and 3 never meet!

More perfect put-downs

• Ever thought of blind dating?
Then you'd only frighten them off with the smell.

• You must be a man of rare intelligence –
either rare or completely extinct!

• Get in training –
I hear 'ugly' is the next Olympic sport!

• Is that your birthday suit?
You should have asked – I could have ironed it for you!

Why do
women
have two
pairs of lips?
**One to talk
to a man and
the other to
shut him
up!**

How to impress
a woman:

- Love her
- Comfort her
- Cherish her
- Protect her
- Kiss her
- Cuddle her
- Listen to her
- Support her
- Compliment her
- Respect her
- Care for her

How to impress a bloke:

- Show up naked
- Bring beer

And finally, still more perfect **put-downs...**

- Tell your trousers it's rude to point!

- I'd love to fuck your brains out, but it looks like someone else got there first!

- You know you've got the body of a god:

  Buddha.

- Tell me everything you know –

  I've ten seconds to spare!

- I'd like to leave you with one thought: one more than you've had all evening.